Awakening Poetry

Awakening Poetry

By
Pam Kegley Warren

Copyright © 2000 by Pam Kegley Warren

All rights reserved.
No part of this book may be reproduced, stored in a retrieval system, or transmitted by any means, electronic, mechanical, photocopying, recording, or otherwise, without written permission from the author.

ISBN: 1-58820-177-5

1stBooks – rev. 8/21/00

The Beauty

Against bends and turns
That most never make
This is a risk
She must take

With an overwhelming determination
She will strive
To do the things
That keep her alive

Like a swan of grace
She does glide
With a touch of class
By her side

She doesn't long for material things
As you and I
But only to feel
The softness from the sky

She sees the beauty of wind
As it brushes her face
And loves the things
Nature brings her way

She clings to many things
Most overlook
Like the emotional parts
In a good book

Although she may never be
A famous model
She has the wisdom
Of a professor in college

With ears sharp and keen
She finds so much beauty
In all that
Her eyes have never seen

The One

I am the one that covers her
When she is cold

The one that teaches her
As she grows

The one that cares for her
When she is ill

And cleans up the messes
No matter how bad I feel

I brush her tiny tears
And try to comfort
All her little fears

The one that sits by her bed
Night after night
To scared to sleep
No matter how tired or how weak

I am the arms that hold her tender
As she cries out in pain
And sometimes I cry with her

The bond between us
And the need to be with her when she is ill

This is a pair of shoes
Only I can fill

I am the one that loves her
More than any other

I am her mother

Who were They?

They were the mothers
That waited for their children
To come home
As the war took them
To depart on their own

They were the mothers
That prayed each night
As their children
Were on the battlefield
Prepared, but so young
To fight

They were the mothers
That dare not go to the door
In fear they would see
Thy children no more

They were the sons
That gave their lives
To never be fathers
Nor to take wives

They were the boys
That came home
As men
Carrying the wounds
Deep within

They were the fathers,
Sons, and husbands
That fought for our country
And for us

The brave soldiers
That gave so much

So please
Remember our Veterans
And their families

A Smile

Sometimes it's so hard to see
Where the foundation of stone was lain

How a person struggles through right and wrong
Yet still they must walk in the rain

The mortar that holds the brick
Must be the heart of the man
And the sweat from his brow
The strength from his hands

The door never closes to the one that gives
From the heart and soul
No matter the bearing of his load

And the window that rests upon the wall
Like a mirror to beauty
It shows him things from afar

And when the weather gets bad
And he cries from within
The roof will be the shelter
That protects him

And in all that he has done
From the carpet to the tile

Sometimes he still has to look deep within
For the power of a smile

Ages of Past

Fingers so fragile they ache
With every move

Skin old and wrinkled
Where much age has shown through

Time went by so quickly
As many mirrors did change images

From deep as darkness to white as snow
Through it now the brush proceeds
Ever so slow

Tainted cheeks that diminished their glow
As gentle beauty faded
So many years ago

Do I dare now stand before the fountain of youth
And take back what is mine

Give to thee the wrinkles that have taken over
My body

And left such sweetness behind

Gulp thy water into my veins
Restoring the fruit
Age has slain

Intensify the pleasure
That still frequents my mind

And grasp a part of my past
The world has left behind

But as does each season come and go
So fast

My younger years are now
Just ages of past…..

She Sleeps

Looking up in the dark
The only sound around
Is the pounding of her heart

The little footsteps start down the hall
Just another drink of water
When mama hears the tiny call

I can't get it on my own
Will you walk with me
So I'm not alone

Lights go out again
She still can't sleep
She counts one, two, and ten

She gives a small tug
Mama she says
I need another hug

Mama will you stay with me?
I'll go to sleep soon you'll see

Now quietly she sleeps
Tucked safely beside of me

Their World

Through the mysteries of their world
Do our little children go

Where ladybugs can sing
And how tall mushrooms can grow

Little monkeys may come to share tea
And often how rude other toys may be

Where birds can talk
And swans of purple can stand up and walk

Colorful candy may fill a room
Where there's no more pizza
Not after noon

Where their favorite cartoon
May leap from t.v.

Don't we wish
This is how simple our lives could be

The Table

The table is still set
Like it used to be
So hard to forget
It was just you and me

Your memory runs through my mind
I'm old and weak now
I have nothing but time

I count the forks each day
None are gone
They're still in place

Each cushion just as it was
No need to move them
They're polished in dust

The Place I Go

I go to a place
Most minds don't know

To the center of another world
I call my own

I can have rain, sun, or snow
I'm the creator
And I'm in control

18

The Gift

That gift that was given
So unexpected
But so sweet of him

The box wrapped
To every perfection
A little big
To avoid detection

The heat rising
Strong into my face
As the explosion of nervousness
Still awaits

Wisely I'll shake it
When he hands it to me
As to question
What ever could it be

The ribbon purposely
Hung in the tree
He knows how anxious
I am to see

Finally, the package
Comes into my hands
God how I love this man

I'll cry when he puts it on my finger
It'll be a moment
Kept always to linger

Quietly I sit
As I patiently open it

Our eyes meet
Just like the movies
This is so neat

Now on to the good stuff
Why do they make this tape
So darn tuff
I close my eyes
While taking the top off

Now I open it quickly
To see
A wrist watch

Some mistake I thought
But he turns to me
And says
I know how much
You needed a watch

As I Watched

I watched through the window
As she held to you
I heard the birds sing
As I felt my heart move

Not understanding why
You were now
Gathered at the door
I sank a little lower
Waiting to see more

Without failure
She had played you
And without caution
You allowed her to

Now you look so
As to be startled

Did she not nurture
Your heart
As you provided the wounds
She stretched the scars

Like an old movie
Playing in the back of my mind
I felt your expression
Cross upon mine

I knew what you were feeling
Because I once felt it too

But somehow as I watched
I felt sorry for you

Destiny

Wonder where you are
When life seems so hard
When the ups never come your way
But the downs seem to stay

When laughter never rings free
And with anger you seem to bleed

When the heart cannot feel love
And you cannot remember what dreams
Are made of

When pleasure turns to pain
And the only clouds you see
Are the ones filled with rain

Destiny may be what you believe
But I see the world
A little differently

It's reaching to the soul
Putting forth an effort
And meeting your goal

Seeing through different eyes
Not letting our mind
Rule our lives

It's giving up the material things
From the start
To find the love our mothers
Bestole in our hearts

It's not going back

To change what is gone
It's finding yourself
And moving on

Our lives are an endless cycle of open doors
And the difference between living and dying
Is what we reach for

I Sit

I sit on a bench in the park

I often wave to the passing cars

I hear the echo of teenagers laugh

As they cruise using main street as their path

To them I am not young

Extremely old is what I am

I wonder do they know

This path is also where my life began

Daddy's

God gave all when he gave Daddy's
To little girls

There was never a bridge you couldn't cross
Or a building you couldn't build

I grew up thinking my Daddy could do anything
And you always proved it was true

And with this you made me believe that
I too could do anything I set my heart to

I am so proud to be your daughter

I love you

I Have Traveled

Without a compass I have traveled
Treaded the waters
Without any paddles

Still I got there on my own
No way to reach me
No telephone

Like a magnet I was drawn
To the sands
And to the dawns

Now the distance seems so long
No hands to guide me back
All the ships are gone

The last vessel sailed the seas
And the cargo carried my heart
Away from me

Now my mind just floats
In my bedroom
I built this boat

Sometimes I hear you in my dreams
Your arms to be my oars
So it seems

But my safety is the shore
And my freedom
Has no door....

Puzzle

Every piece has its place
As does each color have its shade

Entwined together
Each to its own

One place
One space
One home

First Day of School

Her little hands shaking
Mama has to go
Her little heart breaking

She will be brave
And try not to cry
As mama says goodbye

All the kids play and run
But she feels alone
She's not having fun

She takes her doll
Out of her bag
It's not worth much
It was made from a rag

But it warms her heart
While mama's away
And they're apart

The day seems so long
Mama hasn't come back yet
Wonder what's wrong

She taps her tiny feet
On the floor
There's a knock
Is mama at the door?

Remember

No I can't remember
The sound of your voice

My mind has blocked it out
But not by choice

No I can't remember
The depth of the pain

But only the greatness
It's all the same

I do remember
The chills you gave me
As you walked towards me

I remember the pictures
You took
And how I couldn't smile
You wanted them to be perfect
With your own special style

I remember the quietness
As you poured me a drink

My mind wandering
I'd had so much time to think

The way you gently wiped
The drool from my chin

The numbness I felt
As I grinned

I remember how you whispered
Quiet and low
You didn't see me enough
I should visit more

But most of all I remember
When you said we were through

At that moment I knew Doc
You had finally pulled my tooth

Golden Flowers

Golden flowers that cover our earth
Each one bare at its new birth

The eyes of the hour as the sun beams down
Replenishing secrets into the ground

Moonlight is here and buds have came
Tomorrow the warmth of the sun will flourish their veins

The deepest of colors to stain their leaves
Brings us great beauty hard to believe

If only I could have known You

There were so many times when I was lonely
And just needed my mommy to hold me

What I would have given to remember one walk with you
Or to know your arms around me when I felt blue

I wish you could have been there
When I was growing up
I know you my mother
Could have taught me so much

The friends we could have been
What I would give
To have you back again

We could sit up all night long
Watching movies till dawn

I'd tell you secrets I never told my friends
Cause you my mother
Would understand

I'd have you over for dinner
And make you candy in the winter

We'd go Christmas shopping together
Building memories to last forever

We'd laugh over silly things too
Like mothers and daughters often do

Take pictures of our hair in a mess
Arguing over whose looked the best

There's so much I would have given you
If only I could have known you

But these are some of the times I'll never see
And often I wonder
Mommy, why did you leave me

I know you didn't take your heart
You left it behind
Because sometimes I close my eyes and feel it beat in mine

My Day

My trucks loaded down
I'm ready to go
To the lake or the woods
Where I don't know

My guns in the back
My fishing pole too
All my works done nothing more to do

I've waited all week for this day to come
No time to waste
I've got to run

Pulling out of the driveway I look down
Five more minutes
I'll be to town

Dusk is breaking
My needles buried
Blue lights in sight
Man now I'm worried

I pull to the shoulder
As my heart beats faster
My perfect day
Just became a #1 disaster

I wipe the sweat onto my jeans
He's got to be the biggest cop
I've ever seen

"What's the hurry son"
As he comes to my door
You could have heard a pin drop

As I melted to the floor

I told him my story
As he cleared his throat
"This one's a warning," he said
Hitting my coat

I turn around as he turns his head
My clock awakens me
I'm still in bed

Old Moe

I rolled up my sleeves
I could hear old Moe
Trumpeting the leaves

When he hit that bare spot
I'd take my first shot

I raised my gun
He was supposed to stop
Not run

I jumped down from my stand
Hit to my feet
And I ran

I tried to keep up the pace
I was getting tired
As my heart began to race

He looked back as to grin
Just before he rounded the first bend

I fell to my knees
That's when I saw him
Charging through the weeds

He snorted as he pawed the ground
I crept to the cliff's edge
Not making a sound

One leap he was over my head
Still shaking
I thought I was dead

I looked down as he looked up
The last thing he saw
Was my white tail
Heading for the truck

Pearl

Coral around the ocean floor
In a shell you're nested in its door

Your silken beauty enclosed in white
Protected by the seas of the night

Rare secrets do you keep
Like a jewel to creatures far and deep

The tides are up
It's time to leave
The coral opens
You've been released

How freely you float to the shore
Just as if you've been there before

The bright light how it shimmers
Before your eye
As the sunlight seeps in
For just a little while

Now crested in the sand
No longer hidden from the sight of man

Soon your seal will be broken
A gasp heard
No words need be spoken

You'll become a treasure to the outer world
A find specimen
Of a perfect Pearl

The Heart

The heart cannot be measured
By the hours or minutes it grieves

It's a hurt that can last
An eternity

Like a clock with no hands
Yet it can spin its time around any man

An unforgettable memory
That can put you to your knees

Making the strongest man
Turn weak

It's not something you can rewind
To play again

It's a piercing pain that can rip you
From within

See Her

Day after day at suns first light
She came from her home
In a satin gown of white

Virtually motionless
She sat by the ocean side
Her small frame bent forward
She had the body of a child

Her feet lay knowingly in the sand
As the tide shifted
The water came to land

The waves would bounce
Upon her thighs
Without notice
The stare was never broken
From her eyes

So predictable to that same place
Loneliness always bewildered her face

As a statue perched on a stone
She seemed so lost
To thoughts of her own

Until one July morning
They noticed she was gone
People came to huddle
They all gathered round
No trace of her
No body ever found

So they made up their own conclusions

And spread them through the town

Some say she was taken
By the prince of tides
And on a glorious ship
She does ride

Others say
Lost to the greatest wave she did die

But with imagination
Both far and near
Look hard into the ocean
And you too just might see her

This Soldier

Through briers and thickets
And water to the knees

The mouth so dry
He found it hard to breathe

The sun peered between
Scattered clouds

Beads of sweat
Bestow the brows

From night
To the next dawn

Bound to crawling
He would go on

Like an ocean to ones ears
Came the penetration
From his chest

As if the body begging
Give me rest

But he did not stop

No matter how many mountains
He dared to cross

Still came another
And he remained to be lost

Then as darkness

Fell once more

The moon brought forth destiny
To shine upon the earth's floor

The trees parted
And their leaves blew forward

Clearing a path
South of the border
This is where the journey
Would end

Up ahead
This soldier
Would again
Rejoin his men

Who am I?

I bare the children
That help plant the farm
And watch over them
To keep them from harm

I mow the yard
No need to complain
But I am tired

I rake through the weeds
To get the ground ready
To put in the seeds

I have blisters on my hands
But I am strong
Just like a man

On Tuesdays I can for the winter
So when we can't get out
We can still have dinner

My ankles ache
But there's no rest
I have to sew a new slip
To the bottom of my dress

After dark I can't work in the fields
I'm needed in the kitchen
To make sure the tatters are peeled

Can you guess who I am?

I am the farmer's wife

Flame

In a time where there was much shame
They never spoke a word
Not even her name

Cast out into the night
In hopes to be hidden
Not acknowledged in sight

The burning of her heart
She carried through life
Or the presence of her beauty
Each one a threat
To every man's wife

The torch she carried deep inside
For only one man
Would she have given her life

His families power so strong
A poor peasant girl for their son
She was all-wrong

In barefeet she did walk
With a love so many others
Have so often sought

Without his hand
She didst go
But with his heart
She doest forever hold

At night when the stars are all out
Her legend lives on
Beneath a bright cloud

For even in death
Love never died
The flame of passion
Winded the skies

Love is the name

Mother of light to shine
On the flowers

A vision of butterflies
To fill the towers

Heartbreak and stress
Don't linger here

Tender is just a whisper
To all who are near

A kiss in the garden
To subdue the pain

Sweet is the hour
Love is the name

They did flock

The clock impounded in stone
To calm the rivers
They tried on their own

The dove did fly
As they arose from their nest
In gentle splendor
Love would be the test

To exhale into the night
As one breath
They would breathe
As one heart
They would beat

As time did unlock
Above the heavens
They did flock

For twelve years

For twelve years she sat at home by the phone
She gave up her young life and grew old all alone

Her hair now thinning and two shades of gray
What a good come back this old lady will make

So off to the closet for her Sunday best
It's pearls and heels with her red dress

Rollers went up and curls came down
It's into the car and off to town

Her foot not as heavy as it used to be
Now cars are passing in packs of three

Horns are blowing and fists are shaking
Not quiet understanding she smiles and keeps waving

Although to memory some things have changed
The local tavern still bears its sweet name

A room full of kids it doesn't look like it once did
The band is bringing up the two-step
But she's into the twist

The music stopped quickly but she never did
Poor old thing never took a break not even to sit

At a quarter till three it's time to leave
She just can't get the rhythm out of her feet

With her car swerving to the right and to the left
A local cop would make her arrest

They thought she was drunk and hauled her to jail
She had to call her grandson to help make her bail

Twenty aching muscles that couldn't be soothed
For twelve more years she didn't move

His Voice

His voice so nervous
The chin quivered with each word

Not as if his first time speaking
But instead his first time heard

How different for
A man of his age
To stand before us
With so little grace

What is to be scared of
I solemnly thought

It's not as if he wasn't teaching
What he too had been taught

The lump in his throat
I could almost feel its pain

As he gasped for air
From the indubitable strain

Pride

The road is never easy
When a man loses his dignity

Though he stands for what he believes in
Some have never walked where he has been

But is such a great man
That swallows his pride

Even when he feels
As if his soul has died

My little Girl

My little girl came home today
As sad as she could be.

I looked in her soft brown eyes
And asked, "What's wrong with my baby?"

Looking up with tiny tears
She said, "All the kids are making fun of me."

"My shoes are to tight,
My skirts to short
I don't dress well enough
To play with them at all."

That night we went shopping
At a little place with a great big heart
In just a few minutes
We had a full cart.

I sent her back to school the next day
As happy as could be.
She said, "Mom I went in
And they all gathered around me."

"They said my clothes must have cost a lot
I was dressed so nicely.
I told them I got them at Wal-Mart
Laughing quietly."

So here's to all the Wal-Mart's
From mommies just like me

Thanks for all you do for the little shoppers
And God Bless the Family..

The Party

The mind of a boy
In the body of a man
I know I can do it
Cause my age says I can

With a screamin bad headache
An aspirin can't touch
At last night's party I had a little too much

It's not the chase that I'm after
But it always comes
It goes far beyond the drink
That gets me so drunk

And today I can't find the glory
Like I found the guts
One got me started
But it's never enough

The promise I made
In the back of my mind
It slipped through my conscience
Like it does everytime

Now I feel the guilt
As it eats at my pride
This is one thing
Even a big man can't hide

And the morning paper
Lies right where I stand
Oh, God I can't remember last night
Or where I was again

No tragedies through page three
God you must have had your angels
Watching over me

Cause the liquor tempted me
As I drank till I couldn't see
But as usual your arms
Brought me home safely

The Chair

Each little flower painted with care
A beautiful picture of my favorite chair

The memories that are in it
It's been there and back
But it's still my favorite piece
And the best place to sit

If you stare at its arms the koolaid
You will see
I still remember the day
And how she looked at me

But we wiped it all up
While she stood so still
I smiled and with a big kiss
I said, "It's no big deal."

The torn place in the fabric
With scissors she learned to cut
The painter wanted to leave it out
But it means so much

The stories that I told her
Most of them told right there
She'd always drift to sleep
Holding to my hair

When she was big enough
To sit up alone
She never wanted help
She'd climb up on her own

I can still hear her giggle

As she looked back at me
It was the sweetest face
A mama could ever see

She'd place her baby dolls
Up on my lap
Say mama watch over them
While they take their nap

These are the memories
That we all try to hold
If you don't keep them now
You'll forget them
When they're grown

So I hang my picture up
On the wall
My beautiful chair with every little flaw

Our Playhouse

As little kids we did play
Running through the woods
To our special place

Golden lockets blowing in the air
As cute little ribbons hung from our hair

Our playhouse floor molded of bright green moss
It was a whole lot cheaper than carpet would have cost

Doors made of entangled vines
Held together by big white pines

Precut logs with comfort fit
Made great chairs for us to sit

A pretend phone
Made out of an old bottle
We brought from home

A tacky piece of plastic hung overhead on branches
It made a perfect roof
So the rain couldn't catch us

One hundred years ago it seems
This is where we built our dreams

Kittens

Little white kittens
Oh, how they stink
It was out in the mud
And off to the creek

How brave they were
As they neared the bank

The edge gave way
And all three sank

To the top of the water
One at a time
They'd grab to a limb
And out they would climb

Up the hill to safety at last
But a big black dog
Lingered in the grass

His tail like a bulldozer
As it came through the weeds

The three little kittens
Scared as could be

They needed a miracle
And it's just what they got
A herd of deer
Diverted the dog

The three little kittens ran so hard
To get to mama cat who stood in the yard

They didn't even mind
The trouble they were in
As one by one
Mama cat scolded them

Then gently she licked clean their fur
As they rubbed up next to her

Would you?

Would you cry a tear of lonely
For a man you didn't know?

Would you offer your hand to someone
If you thought he was cold?

Would you play to the end
Even if you thought you'd lose?

Would you give in to love
Though your heart refused?

Would you?

The Redheaded Cat

The redheaded cat
Where does he lurk?

Up through the pastures
And down in the dirt

The scent of mice to his nose
The smell gets stronger as he gets close

The red hair stands upon his back
His legs perched ready for attack

In fear of danger
They scurry about
Escaping the claws of the stranger

In his confusion the cat stands still
He didn't catch them this time
But one day he will

One to ten

One little boy sits on a bench

Two little marbles he does clinch

Three little girls come to say

Four of us now we can play

Five more boys come up the block

Six little boys is what we've got

Seven people stop to watch

Eight dollars is what they drop

Nine little children sit on a bench

Ten more minutes the game will end

Fish Tank

To clean the fish tank he does go
Into the living room with a great big bowl

A curious toddler Mom don't know
He's got the water way to cold

He sticks his hand in his pocket and pulls out a fork
Chasing them around is such hard work

Maybe if he feeds them they'll be still
He grabs the bread bag and pulls out a heal

The water is so cloudy now he can't see
He sits the bowl in the floor and gets on his knees

This won't do he's got to think
He runs to the bathroom and stops up the sink

He takes both bowls dumping them in
Now they all have room to swim

The fish hit the water and go into shock
Now they all come to the top

He thinks it's funny how they want to float
He sticks in some cardboard to make them a boat

So much excitement he's got to rest
He leaves them in the bathroom
And goes off to bed

Jayse's Lullaby

Little one it's time to sleep
Close your eyes and drift to dream

Tiny fingers wild and free
A little bit of rest is what they need

Little one it's time to sleep
Close your eyes and drift to dream

To mommie's arms you will wake
From a night that's gentle, warm and safe

Now Jayse sleeps
Oh, so silently
Little lashes start to flow
As away to toy land you will go

Chocolate bunnies pave the way
To big candy castles they have made
And little smiles begin to grow
It's off to sleep you go

Morning

The fresh smell of coffee
Lines the morning air

As I feel the heaviness of my lids
Ever so tired

With my feet to the floor
The draft of winter seeps under my door

Frost covers the windows
As I wipe a place to see

The fresh born snow
Shining in front of me

The birds snuggle in their nest
As the bears hibernate for a winter of rest

Looking back

We have come upon troubled times
Although through many we have traveled
But none of this kind

Maybe we weren't listening
When we needed to be

Or maybe through our stress
We just didn't see

It seems that things have happened so fast
We were always looking ahead
When maybe
We should have been looking back

The Artist

He held the palette as if his hands were
Painting their last

So cautious to every movement
As he captured his past

His passion arose
As every hint of emotion he showed

He expressed the wildness
He had once felt

Compelling the eagerness
His hands had held

He painted her as though
She was his very own masterpiece

Far beyond any beauty
The world had ever seen

The whites of her eyes
As pure as the clouds above him

The green, greener than the pastures
Surrounding him

Her lips as red as the last fallen apple
Tumbling from the tree

With every minute pulling from his heart
A great honesty

At last it was a picture of the woman

He had loved so long

The artist now saddened
He cried a tear for what was gone

Promise

Will you forget me in the morning
When you are up and I am gone

Or will I linger through your nights
And awake to your dawns

Will I be the heart that beats
That be stills your everyday

The one true thing
You know love brought your way
As I leave, I leave you with a promise
That I am forever
Though the hands can never hold

I will be your shelter
When you are lonely I will be your soul

Just promise you'll never look for me
Cause I'll be inside your heart

The one that melts the cold through winter
And nourishes the memory

I am the wind that will wake you
And bring warmth to your dark

I will be the reflection in your mirror
When you are old and I am weak

And when time is of no more
I will be the one that helps you go forth

I am the promise we will never part
I am the secret that lives in your heart

My Faith

My faith in you
Made you a man

I believed in all good
To come from your hands

How proper from a boy you had been taught
Never to deceive what you had so long sought

Through sadness you built courage
And when you found triumph
It brought forth marriage

And in all the years that we loved
Not once was I disappointed
Or did I ever lose trust

Ice

I cut a hole
Where ice was froze

I reach in to provide warmth
Where there was cold

I brought my chisel
For it was hard as stone

But even the chisel
Couldn't penetrate it alone

I spoke sweet words
To help melt the shield

But the covering clinched
Tighter still

It was then that I felt failure
And my intent became pure

As the salt water raced from my eyes
So did the echo of loneliness my heart had cried

The glacier broke from its freeze
And his hand opened for me

Mom

For nine months you carried me
Deep within your womb
I put you through a hot summer of misery
As I grew till there was no more room

You withstood the pain of labor
For your little girl
And after hours you delivered
Me into this world

From a baby to an adult
You gave me so many gifts
But the greatest
Was true friendship

You taught me from a child
I would never be alone
No matter how far
I traveled from home

And you showed me
That love wasn't what money could buy
It was tenderness
From a mother to her child

Through the years
You have brought me so much happiness
As I discovered
God couldn't have given me
A more perfect mother

You are the best

Rose

You sent a fresh cut rose
Its petals will wilt soon I'm told

The stem most amazing
You swore it was crystallized
By loves imagination

You enclosed a little note
One from your soul I'd hoped
And my heart was in a daze

For a moment I took it to extremes
Lace to flesh as I dreamed

The days turned to years
And as each passed by
I noticed its petals
Began to die

What was once such splendor
Now lay alone
It couldn't even help I'm sorry
As it darkened our home

It lasted so much longer
Than many may have thought
Even a perfect flower
Still has its faults

As angry words echoed
Through closed doors
The crystal rose
Shattered upon the floor

I've heard

I've heard the ivy
As it crawls onto my legs
Begging for attention
As it spreads

I've heard the trees
As they release air onto the leaves
Dusting them gently with their sneeze

I've heard the fish
As they saunter through the streams
Beneath the clear water as it gleams

I've heard the sun
As it shines on my face
Unfolding heat from its rays

I've heard the wolves
From the top of the hill
Crying from hunger as they roam the fields

I've heard the cry of lonely
From your back porch
Filled with tears
I've heard your hurt

The Favor

She places her hands together and she begins to pray
She doesn't usually ask for much
But tomorrow is a special day

"Dear God,
I know I cannot feel the rocks beneath my feet
As I cover my legs I cannot feel the heat
But I'm still praying that you may give me a chance
Let me feel the pleasure of just
One dance."

Her mother stands outside her bedroom door
"Dear God,
Allow her what she prays for."

The hours pass and to the next morning she does wake
But still there's no feeling
No movement from her legs

Prom hour isn't far
As her father carries her to the car

She asks him to drop her off and then go ahead
When she gets ready she'll go in and dance

She peeks through the window where she sits
As tears begin to fall upon her dress

She realizes she has no way to get her chair
To the top of the steps

But Tommy's not far
With a handful of flowers
He takes her in

As the band plays a song
Someone requested for them

He pushes back her chair
With a smile full of charm
As he takes her into his arms

About the Author

I remember picking up a pen and writing my first poem around the age of ten. At that time in my life writing was not that important. It was just something to do when I was bored. As I got older I realized God had given me a very special gift and I had the ability to use it. I began to find a pleasure in writing I couldn't find anywhere else. There was a whole different world waiting in my imagination and all I had to do was write it down. From poetry to songs it didn't matter as long as I was writing. I now write whenever the words hit my mind. Often there are times I wake up in the middle of the night and grab a pen and pad and write in the dark so I don't wake anyone else. Sometimes it's funny because when I wake up the next morning I often wonder where the thoughts came from.

I owe special thanks to my wonderful parents for always believing in me and helping me to understand sometimes you have to believe in yourself to make your dreams come true. To my husband and children for sharing me with my work and being the great critics they are. Along with my aunts, uncles, family and friends, these are the people that helped push my dream into reality.